Under the Sign of the Samovar

poems of seven decades

Marcia Katz Wolf

Plain View Press, LLC   www.plainviewpress.net
1101 West 34th Street, Suite 404, Austin, TX 78705

Copyright © 2015 Marcia Katz Wolf. All rights reserved under International and Pan-American Copyright Conventions. No part of this book may be reproduced or distributed in any form or by any means, or stored in a data base or retrieval system, without written permission from the author. All rights, including electronic, are reserved by the author.

ISBN: 978-1-63210-017-7
Library of Congress Control Number: 2015945678

Cover art: photographs permission of Marj Green
       "Samovar" ©2010 Tom & Marj Green
       "Pitcher and Lace" ©2010 Tom & Marj Green
       website: www.tomandmarj.com
Cover design by Pam Knight

For Irving

Contents

My grandmother's samovar   7

1945-1963: Home Permanent   9
The Samovar   11
The Dread of Coming Home   12
Home Permanent   13
Jewels in the Five & Dime   14
Do No Harm   15
Little Miss Muffet, or Esau's Revenge   16
The Birthmark   17
Lear, Father   18

1964-1982: About Mary   19
Lewis Carroll, Notwithstanding   21
About Mary   22
Mine   23
For Mac McCurdy Dead of Huntington's Chorea   24
Dream   25
The Child   26
According to the DSM   27
At Yoga   29
On a Day I Was Mad   30
A Truth Widely Accepted   31

1982-2000: Autumn Tricks   33
Last Night   35
Autumn Tricks   36
Oncologist   37
On Ramona Street   38
Registering   39
At a Time When Truth   40
Pain   41
Poems   42
The Gift of Feet   43

You Tell Yourself	44
I Believe in Make-Up	45
Anything Goes	46
Nicholas T. Sheley	47
My Husband Is a Patient Man	48
For Jennie, Once More	49
And to the Republic, for Witches Stand	50
Philip	51
Stopped at the Light	52
December 6	53
Gogol's Overcoat	54
First Thoughts of Morning	55
John Donne, Revisited	56
In the Living Room	57
For Yonatan, Born December 13, 1999	58

2000-2015: Even Now   59

Euphemisms	61
Tabula Rasa	62
As My Birthday	63
Old Age	64
Moriturus	65
If I Could Ask My Father	66
Lullaby	67
Are You a Narcissist?	68
Walking With Mika	69
Sports Cars	70
Dancing With Anna	71
Counterparts	72
Utilitarianism, Redux	73
In the Beginning All Over Again	74
Mika at 14 Months	75
Pilgrim Soul	76
Anna's Tricycle	77
Even Now	78

About the Author	81

My grandmother's samovar has been an abiding presence in my life. Carried to the United States as she and my great-grandparents escaped the Russian pogroms, it is a reminder of their determination to resist the forces that seek to destroy the human spirit, their courage in leaving behind all they had known. In losing their home, they made it possible for my parents to find ours. I have written these poems to tell my children what the samovar has told me:

We cannot separate what we've lost from what remains. It is together that they take us home.

1945-1963:
Home Permanent

My grandfather and grandmother, Charles and Minnie Bernstein, in front of their house in Plymouth, Wisconsin.

My grandmother Minnie holding me and my mother Anne holding my brother Daniel in our grandparents' back yard.

The Samovar

My grandfather home for supper from the salvage yard,
dawdling on the front porch in his overalls,
sipping tea from my grandmother's samovar
the old Russian way, sugar cube between his teeth—
shadows move across the cornfields beyond our house,
he watches as light and mood pass—
fifty years later, visiting my sister in Madison,
we drive to Plymouth to find that house.
But no one in the family can remember the address,
so we drive for awhile, aimlessly, when out of no where
it comes to me: 20 Edna Street—
we ask directions, drive a few blocks and there it is:
pale yellow clapboard duplex, freshly painted,
next door, an elderly woman watering her lawn
looks up, smiles, "Are you looking for someone?"
"My grandparents, Minnie and Charlie Bernstein—
they lived here a long time ago. I'm Marcia."
"What do you know? Wasn't that you with the long dark braids
and your little red-headed cousin who used to visit from Minneapolis?
Well, everything fades. Some fast, some slow. Red hair's a fast one.
We're lucky ours used to be black."

The Dread of Coming Home

Leaving my bright school room for the cold light
of the Minneapolis winter afternoon,
worried about what I'll find when I get home,
I look to the trees along the parkway,
aspen, maple, horse chestnut, for their stolid reassurance—
my mother, calling down to me to keep her company
as she lies in her bath, relaxed and rhapsodizing
about the Russian Revolution, her hero, Trotsky,
her favorite writers, Auden, Emerson, George Eliot,
or, having had a fight with my father the night before,
will she be in her basement sewing room,
rough cement walls, cracked linoleum, one small, high window—
I'll be invisible to her as she feverishly cuts
the dark material around the pattern,
bits and pieces falling to the floor,
then her foot on the treadle,
the needle begins its slow puncturing, in and out, in and out,
and holding up to the window what she's finished,
as though it were my father she's finally gotten in shape,
unable to see in the fading light
what has already begun to unravel.

Home Permanent

The first time my mother left

my father lying next to me at nap time,

I was five. He asked, "What can I do

to make you happy again?"

"Cut my braids (they were down to my waist)

so my hair can be curly, like on television."

"Then you'd be the twin with the Tony," he smiled—

"Your hair is too straight."

So he cut them off,

but never did find time for the permanent.

Jewels in the Five & Dime

Flaming, cooling, growing crystal-like

Into the Emerald City—

Tears transubstantiated

In Woolworth's.

Come, says Ali Baba.

They gleam.

Here, says Aladdin.

Follow me, I say to my cousin Laura

Who smirks at the

Emeralds glistering, sapphires, diamonds—

My Aunt Pearl having taking us after Sunday School

To buy me Modess,

Sticky redness spreading

Under my Sunday best.

Do No Harm

Once I knew a man, a doctor,
who a year after he returned from the Second World War
had a son. This boy displayed from the time he was young
a tremor in both hands.
When his father would come home from the lab,
frustrated, worn down, an unwelcome test result,
another grant proposal rejected—
he would ask something of the boy, older now,
to pour a drink, carry it into the den without spilling it,
and when, for an instant, the boy held his breath,
closed his eyes to conjure the quivering liquid,
his father would shout, "Stop that shaking!"
then haunted in the middle of the night by the boy's terror of him.
Had he not gone to the war, might his vision of his son
have been rather of life, wind blowing through his hands,
the beating of a heart, or wings—
perhaps then he might not have, with his steady surgeon's hands,
stopped the shuddering of his own heart,
might instead have lived long enough to see his son
with his ear to the root
of all that trembles.

Little Miss Muffet, or Esau's Revenge

Has any child ever liked Miss Muffet?
Me, personally, I always rooted for the spider,
just the way I liked Esau best, his hunger and soft hair—
and who would hang around with anybody
who would hog something
that resembles cottage cheese?
So I voted for the spider—
loved his chutzpah, sitting down,
not at the back of the tuffet but, it said,
right beside her.
And much later, it was a great relief
to learn about karma and reincarnation
(the end of that Bible story so unsatisfactory),
because then I realized that Mother Goose's Jacob,
gets his just deserts,
so now I will forever see Jacob fleeing in lace,
and the hairy hunter alone at last
with every curd
& all the whey.

The Birthmark

My Grandmother called me Shena Medl, pretty girl
as if with frosting she made me
and called my father to the table, the doctor,
whose spinning eye fixes me
raised finger like a knife-tip
shivers my nose:
"I could do the job right here,"
and he winks—"The blade is warm,
slips easy through the soft flesh, like butter melting"—
   But my husband loves me through my make-up, 'Imagine:
      pale lashes stirring
         spheres converge, sockets fall back
            to where cheek bone
               cascading down'—

Lear, Father

1.
They say he bummed cigarettes
on and off all that live long day
and moved
machine to machine
match flare and burn, Hosannah
mark the act of consumption
2.
my last day home
I ironed,
you in the blue bathrobe
"My children don't need me
anymore."
3.
the presence of the heart, Father,
is not a secret
you dispatch
crack, see where the dry sand breeds
4.
        no no no, father
        you may not eat your daughter
        the warp'd belly for to puff and grow
        such labor's not in order
        else the cuckoo reigns below
5.
all day he moved
with the roar of the machine
no place
no place to rest
hum the machine with his head
sweet head, lay it down
it was Friday dusk
and he died
fittingly

1964-1982:
About Mary

Lewis Carroll, Notwithstanding

I have a sorrow, Mother

I have a sorrow, Father

I'm caught over here

in the Looking Glass—

Stranded above

Drowned below

I'm left for right

In the Mirror Zone

About Mary

Every Jewish Mother's
Nightmare:
With no input from any body
She bears the Messsiah
(To savor)
Then the Goyim
Destroy Him.

Thus, every Jewish Mother's
Burden:
To greet her children
As if they had not just risen
From the dead.

Mine

I bend down
between my baby's hands
head against warm stomach
heat rising, like a hearth
breath so close it is almost my own

She keeps her secret well
my child
smells so sweet.

And if I calculate the velocity of breath
times the brow's heat
will I find the meridian
of that seed?

For Mac McCurdy Dead of Huntington's Chorea on Memorial Day, 1979

That night my husband reading from Leviticus,
"...and if his means suffice not
for two turtle doves..."
"How beautiful" I said
and fell asleep

      early morning.
the call   .   Mac dead in his car

so quiet   .   his hands on my daughter's head
eyes lowered, hiding
the father's disease
like birds pecking

                        hands stately on the wheel swinging
                        around / rudder of that great boat
                         to that oak

                                There is no choice?
                                Grieve instead for the ram

                        its horns locked in the thicket.

Dream

Boats all that morning came
to take us far away
schooners, sloops and sailing ships
kayaks and canoes
when a silver disk skimmed toward me
like a whirling chafing dish
to spin me up and serve me
to the pale and silent sea
as cold and flat and endless
as my father's leaden eye.
But a friend and I went skipping
above the glassy waves
and a sandbar rose beneath us
like a gently guiding hand—
Houses bright with open doors
sprouted up and down the shore
fragile teacups waiting
sweaters filling drawers
sapphire, amber ocher, rose
feathered sequined, shimmering clothes,
and in our glee we chortled
for neither of us cared
that all the rest had gone and drowned
in that ocean over there.
Bottoms bob like muffins
pummeled by the tide
then carried down and deeper down
in my father's moonstone eye.

The Child

The child under her arm
hanging loosely
chambers of water rising—
She says to him,
"It is sweet to die."
He says, "The fault is your daughter's,
she found the oil that was poison,
that befouled the boat and its inner workings,
but you thinking it seaworthy,
sailed on."

According to the DSM[1]

If three or more of the following apply to you:
1. You sing your children lullabies tho they are older than you when they were born;
2. You still cut their bagels to keep them from severing an artery;
3. You go to K-Mart to buy them a bumpy rubber mat so they won't slip in the shower and suffer a head injury;
4. While there you pick up two extra smoke alarms, just in case;
5. You worry that their brakes might fail;
6. Or their mates;
7. Or that they will buy a house near a levee or a fault line;
8. Last night in a dream you saw Pharaoh's daughter

> stopping by the river
> in the heat of the day
> watching a rocking basket,
> water lapping over a sleeping child
> river nudging it back and forth—
> then with greater force, pushing and pulling,
> when, suddenly, summoning all its strength,
> the river inhales, and as the basket
> drops into the pure hollow,
> Pharaoh's daughter continues on her way, unseeing
> as dark eyes snap open, close, and open again,
> lashes beating like the flagella of a soft sea creature,
> here for an instant and then gone—

continued...

---

1 Diagnostic and Statistical Manual of Mental Disorders

Then you are suffering from Maternal Attachment Disorder (or MAD),

    and after your morning coffee and newspaper,
    you will drive to an appointment
    when for 50 minutes, no more, and no less,
    you lie balanced on a fine leather couch with your eyes closed,
    high above the brink
    of the sea.

At Yoga

Lying on the floor, my legs splayed,
the Yoga teacher says,
"Imagine what you most truly and deeply desire"—
'Big Bucks,' I think, alarming myself (I have never lived for Money),
when just then, a voice in my head whispers, 'Yo Men,'
and appearing on a hill in the distance
Bambi's father, imperial,
chest and flanks glistening,
antlers, huge trees,
branches sharp enough to slice the atom,
breath coiling upward into a mushroom cloud,
or the exploding universe, hundreds of thousands of years
before there was light,
billions of years before either the atom or I
had been split.

On a Day I Was Mad

I saw sitting on a park bench
a tall man with shaggy red hair
turning into an large orange cat
grooming himself in a pool of sunshine—
Now that I am sane again
I still see him on his bench
and though I try to spot some clue to his feline past
all I ever see is a bedraggled old man
staring off into space—sans fur, sans tail
sans rough tongue
to smooth and comfort.

A Truth Widely Accepted

The punishment brewing
in the roots of that tree, so we've been told,
was not just time,
or exile with hard labor,
or the doomed longing for goodness—
but choice,
at each instant,
every turning,
choice upon choice.
Not to mention that infamous fruit
taking its pick
to fall
all the way down.

1982-2000:
Autumn Tricks

Last Night

Last night I dreamed my husband left me

for a woman 30 years younger—

I asked, How can you stop loving?

This cold November morning

he's gone to his weekly shopping

and I to my house cleaning,

sweeping away today

and the earth,

as its attention dwindles,

its spirit shrinks.

Autumn Tricks

Dazzling fall afternoon

  Not wanting to blot it

    With my darkness

I apply to the stains

  Above and below my eyes

    A pale, slightly iridescent pink powder

Holding this bright face before me

  I step off my shaded porch

    Twinned in mirthful recognition

      Of what only the shadows know.

Oncologist

As she prepared to greet

the new stage 4 pancreatic cancer,

she intoned to herself again

If I can't kill it, I don't care about it,

extending her slim hand

to the 71-year-old college professor

with neatly trimmed hair

and blue, blue eyes.

On Ramona Street

Yesterday I was window-shopping on Ramona Street

when walking briskly toward me, a bespectacled

man in a sweat suit and running shoes slowed, peered at me sharply,

then hurried on his way—

Flattered at first, it didn't take me long to realize

that what he actually saw, it is impossible to know—

It could have been someone of any age, gender, or even species,

just as he to himself might have been skimming the pavement

in shiny dancing shoes

and a high top hat.

Registering

Volunteering at the food bank,

I ask the next person in line,

Are you registered here?

What do I have to do to register? See

Where this tooth used to be?

Can you count that?

Okay, then, what about that I had

Just enough hope left

To wait all day in your long line?

At a Time When Truth

is a delusion

religion, spite

politics, plotting

and love, an agglomeration of hormones

sloth is my philosophy

sleep my consolation

but I will try to help you tidy up,

(just as soon as I've had my nap).

Pain

Yesterday I gashed my foot

on the sharp edge

of an open drawer—

The pain beat at me

knocked me down,

I thought, this is good. Keep it coming.

Color this drab morning unreeling like a blank tape

from bland to bloody.

Poems

Lately they come after the sun goes down

swilling in darkness, tumescent

swans slow-dancing across a dusky stage

Nazis in bunkers digesting still

metabolizing in perfect obedience to nature

and parental ordinance:

Feed silently

Mouth closed.

The Gift of Feet

I thank God for the gift of feet

and where they are attached

so that what ages least, I see most:

pale skin, oval nails

plump digits nestled one beside the other

hint of tender darkness between—

O root of my route

my gorgeous source

flutter me like a cloud

through the open gate.

You Tell Yourself

it takes just the right

light to see

what's really there—here

where the spidery veins appear

(or the downy arm of J. Alfred's lady)—

but what is light, beyond

the tale of our eyes turning

tricks?

I Believe in Make-Up

I believe in make-up,
it's what keeps me sane,
with a breathing tube wound round my neck
and my feet in chains,
I shamble to the mirror
to calm my seething brain,
see more place than face,
a ghost town, dilapidated, grey,
all of me that remains
in one piece, mostly, familiar—

Taking the pink-tipped wand
from the dresser to reinforce my mouth
requires I quell the shouts, the chattering, the doubts—
(perhaps that moan was not my own),
but the sine qua non to dispel the terror
is the patient application of mascara,
layer upon layer enclosing pale lashes,
thick bars to keep in tears
and out derision,
in my impregnable
L'Oreal prison.

Anything Goes

Scratching out words
for a poem that won't go
when my husband interrupts
newspaper in hand—
I look up, irritated; he, abashed,
says, "Here, I have something for you,
nobody could make this up:
the man we killed in Afganistan Sunday—
you know, one of the top Taliban guys—
his name was Mullah Dadulla."
Thus, pleased by my smile, all was restored:
"It sings, doesn't it?"
he says, walking back to the kitchen,
a spring in his step.

Nicholas T. Sheley

On the front page of the San Francisco Chronicle this morning
Nicholas T. Sheley, pictured as he is taken
from the Granite City, Ill. Police Department,
having bludgeoned to death a 93-year-old man,
a 29-year-old man, a 25-year-old man,
a 20-year-old woman and her two-year-old daughter.
"He could have been using a club, a bat,
a crowbar, we don't know—"
said the Chief of Police of Festus, Mo.
In the photo, a cop on either side of Nicholas,
each holding an upper arm, flesh giving way under their grip,
fingers of one against Nicholas's right inner elbow,
neatly trimmed nails and a wedding ring.
Later, lying beside my granddaughter at nap time,
she brushes a lock of hair out of my eyes,
and I think again of Nicholas—
Who welcomed his touch when he was four?
And of his lethal face—fierce, and wounded, and lost—
nose and cheekbones of the "David," my Katz cousins' Slavic eyes,
a face that when I was 16
I could have fallen in love with.

My Husband Is a Patient Man

My husband is a patient man,
schooled in uncertainty, a scientist
used to disappointment,
calm when things don't work out,
cautious when they do—
though by now he must be tired of my moods,
weary of the naggings:
Stand up straight!
Where's your hearing aid?
Another crossword puzzle?
But, frankly, I am stumped
by why he doesn't put his time to better use,
concocting, for example, a potion
to transform a fretful wife,
from particle
to wave.

For Jennie, Once More

Having avoided the house of my neighbor with Alzheimer's

for almost a year, I recently found myself on Jenny's doorstep

and rang the bell—

her husband opened the door, she behind him, expectant:

"How did I live without you?"

Then he: "You're just in time for our celebration.

Next week she's having cataract surgery

so she can play the piano again, her show tunes."

As soon as he disappeared, Jenny whispered to me,

"When I'm by myself, I still play the piano.

We all need a secret thing we do.

 It's what takes us home."

And to the Republic, for Witches Stand

What he said

was "lying

and cheating"

what I wrote

was "lion's cheek"—

spike heels,

a warm bath,

a poem—

all I know

of reincarnation

Philip

When Philip was a newborn
I held him in my arms,
walked with him and sang every lullaby I knew:
Welsh, Appalachian, French
and my favorite, the Indonesian, "Suliram,"
until he fell asleep.
But he was, officially, my step-grandson,
and, so, little by little,
backward step by step, the distance—
Now he is 15, and I bring him offerings:
$25 when he visited in November,
$50 in December, and on his birthday, $150
for half of a very cool bike.

The night before he came to stay with us a few months ago,
my husband and I listened to a short story on NPR
about a chimp who was taught American Sign Language.
When her baby died she held him for many days,
signing "Come Baby Hug."
The story ends, "The chimp had learned human grief."
Of what else had been lost to her, there was no mention,
as she begged her child to come back,
in a foreign language.

Stopped at the Light

Stopped at the red light at Cowper and Forest,
I saw sitting at the bus stop
an elderly woman with crimped hair
the color of cooking oil.
She caught me looking at her
and ran one hand through her bangs,
propping them up on her forehead,
then I knew that as soon as she turned 18,
her father sent her to the best plastic surgeon in Hollywood
to cut out the bump on her nose.
He fashioned an inverted comma in the air
to demonstrate the finished product,
and she said, forcing back tears,
"Can't you just shave off just little?"
Before she knew it, he was on the phone:
"Yale, she's not ready for this,"
and as she closed the door behind her,
"Too bad, you could have been a pretty girl."

December 6

In the dark of the early morning
on the 45th anniversary of my father's death,
in my kitchen preparing two poems for an editor,
I opened the oven door to serve him two chicken breasts,
golden brown, done to perfection, crisp on the outside, tender inside.
"Delectable," he said. "I'll take them."
But as I hesitated, afraid they would fall apart
if I took them off the rack,
an intruder broke down the door
began to assault a young girl who had just appeared in the room.
I attacked him and he knocked me to the ground,
thrust a knife through my hand,
my writing hand, blood soaking the rug.

I read somewhere that a famous poet
said it is through writing poetry that we endure,
but she is only half right.
No matter how tasty the breast, it begins in blood
and blood ends it.

Gogol's Overcoat

I had always remembered Akakiy Akakievitch
freezing to death after his new overcoat was stolen
at midnight on a dark Petersburg street—
the coat for which he starved himself,
going without food, candles,
firewood to warm himself—
his cries unheeded as the coat was wrenched from him,
growing chilled, then numb, then falling asleep,
blanketed by the unending snow—
but the truth I recently discovered
as my husband read the story to me again
is that he really died some days later,
his pleas rebuffed by an indifferent official,
now even his old cloak useless as the fever consumed him.
"Unbearable," says Gogol. "You want consolation. Okay,
I'll give you Akakiy Akakievich's lonely ghost
lifting an overcoat from the shoulders of that very same official,
then ebbing into the fog of the endless night—
or, on second thought, perhaps it was just an ordinary thief—"
Either way, we get no more protection
than from an old coat worn gossamer thin.

First Thoughts of Morning

odd is to the man and where he ripens
sings the waking brain
pulse and thread like an amoeba
within the bounds of justice
Empedocles argued the void away
lifting the skin
found four elements straining
up from my dreams comes the ape in me
wrist and elbow strong
hand over hand in the trees of those savannahs
riding my birth wheel
it is a perfect circle
and I
black fire beneath the skin
drop dark spheres
and it melts
inevitable night
there is no void
none in the inflated skin
man is mind
with hands
that is all.

John Donne, Revisited

What kind of a world have you made
in which we age so publicly
and stay young so privately?
Wouldn't it have been kinder
the other way around?
Our real self, what we are to our self
in the open, vivid still in our yearnings,
the chilling, hardening, hidden from view
sensed only dimly, as if from far away—
There were nights long ago in our house in Minneapolis
when after everyone had fallen asleep
you could hear from the inky darkness of Lake Calhoun
ice growing, the lake's muffled groanings—
Are you listening, You who deemed it so?
Save your breaking and burning for Donne—
As for me, just turn me inside out.

In the Living Room

As my mother was dying, her children and grandchildren
gathered in the living room, Claire turned to me:
"Grandma made me carroway meatballs and mandelbrot,
and, Mom, do you remember
that lemony teacake of hers? It had a special name."
I didn't remember that, but what I did remember
was her nibbling Claire's ear when she was a little girl,
those perfect, pink shells—
"What do they taste like, Grandma?"
"Um, let's see, butterscotch, mostly."
"Really?"
"With, perhaps, just a hint of hot buttered rum,
no, actually—now I've got it! Wild strawberries!"
And sitting in the backyard the summer after Emily was born,
touching the crease in the bend of her plump, brown, arm:
"See, Marcia—there—the color of a peach
just under its leaf."

For Yonatan, Born December 13, 1999

    Bare

        trees

            to tresses

        uprising

of leaf.

2000-2015:
Even Now

Euphemisms

People don't 'pass away' or 'pass on'
    or even merely 'pass,' gliding by
        like Moiseyev dancers
        or discreet waiters—
Nor do they 'transition'—dematerializing
    to be reconstituted
        like astronauts' rations
        in a heavenly sphere
They die.
They cease.
They end.
They stop.
            It is only the Pale Horse who passes.

Tabula Rasa

My children do not see
that I'm disappearing
word by word:
first the name,
then the thing named
gone blank,
that bit of me—
Yesterday, I had to ask Claire:
You know, that sticky stuff
that holds things together?
The rest of the day I wandered around
intoning, Velcro, Velcro,
as if invoking the divine presence—
but I know soon that too will be gone for good
and with it the memories of all the children's shoes
I've fastened on the way to school, or soccer practice, or the park.
Then the day will come when one of these same children,
taking her turn to visit,
trying to help me out of bed,
will raise the sheet and see
that it's all been erased
like an etch-a-sketch.

As My Birthday

As my birthday approaches & winter

each night I lie in bed

and practice dying

(to get the hang of it)

wondering when I awake

just what it is I've wasted, rehearsing

what comes naturally.

Old Age

walking back and forth

year after year

peering into the crib

of the kidnapped child

to see if finally

it has been returned.

Moriturus

When I die, he said

There'll be rules:

No tears

No clinging

No sobs

Nothing to poach on my death

Complicate the dark.

If I Could Ask My Father

"The only thing I know of
that separates human beings
from animals is suicide,"
I would say to my father
had he lived.
"Why is that, Dad?"
"Perhaps," a deliberate thinker, he would pause—
"Perhaps only humans feel shame."
"But," I say, "Koko the gorilla hangs her head
when she makes a mistake on her keyboard."
"Well, then, maybe it's just people who hate themselves."
Would that I had been born a different creature—
macaw, wildebeast—
then I might not have outlived him by 50 years—
shark even, turtle or worm—
anything but human.

Lullaby

I think I would gladly die

if I could sing myself

to sleep, "Sally Gardens,"

"Buttermilk Hill,"

'and every tear would turn a mill'—

until all the tears are gone

and there's nothing left

but song.

Are You a Narcissist?

Are you a narcissist

if before taking the pills

you apply just a touch of lipstick, blush

and mascara, but only on the top lashes

since your eyes

(you hope)

will be closed?

Walking With Mika

Walking down Ross Road with my two-year-old granddaughter,
we come to a half-built-house—
a few men sitting on cement blocks, eating,
chatting in Spanish, others behind them on stubbled grass—
trying to look friendly as I go by,
no one, I think, smiles back and I speed up to the house next door,
ranch-style of indeterminate color,
where in the yard, a field of poppies—
and as the breeze picks up, they lean and sway,
blue and yellow and purple, a corps de ballet of poppies,
swan poppies bending their long necks toward my grandchild.
"Look, Mika,
the flowers are dancing for you"—
then laughter next door, as if mocking, and I step to leave,
but she will not budge—
the wind comes again and the flowers ripple and fold,
almost to kneeling and the laughter unfurls,
weaving itself into the flowers, streaming waves of voice and color—

Eventually we continue on our way,
and when after a few more blocks, we turn back towards home,
pass again the men, absorbed now in their work,
I notice on the fence a sign I had missed
the first time by: Chrisman Construction—
then I know why everything is laughter
and dancing for Mika
and me
on this new May morning.

Sports Cars

There is a prominent doctor who lives close by,
quite amiable, it seemed to me,
though a colleague of his
says "He's full of himself"—tall, charming,
a little asymmetrical, a little dangerous—
I liked his jaunty red sports car,
older, too, but shiny—
then one day I came upon him, distressed,
peering at the engine of a new Porsche,
which closed out my interest for a while,
until yesterday when I saw streaking down El Camino
a silver Porsche winking in the sun,
filled with himself.

Dancing With Anna

In this week of my granddaughter's birth,
as I walk our neighborhood,
the rhododendrun next door just beginning to bud,
small Tulip Tree around the corner on Kingsley with tiny green shoots
under which sits Blossom the tortoise shell cat,
boys, freed from school, singing out at the top of their lungs—
every budding, mewing, shouting being with Anna's face,
and later back at home we dance to "You Send Me"
(because she already has a thing for Sam Cooke),
then as we dip and sway with Belefonte's "Calypso,"
her eyes begin to close to "Brown Skin Girl,"
I'm 'Millie' and she's my 'blue-eyed baby.'

Counterparts

One chilly afternoon a few days before Christmas,
mending by the fire a pillow I had long ago covered
in a bright African print of giraffes, antelopes, and zebras,
as inviolable in their savannah, it had seemed,
as the lovers on Keats's urn,
now suffering a multitude of depredations,
missing pieces of ear, tail, antler, flank
from years of use and abuse as weapons and forts,
Irving reading to me the story of another ruined life
in Joyce's pitiless Dublin—
then the last line: the child pleading with his drunken father
to stop beating him.
Shaken, I look up from my mending at Irving—
He doesn't say to me "It's only a story."
He says, "It's so sad.
All that cruelty.   All that shame."

Utilitarianism, Redux

If in your philosophy, Jeremy,

the lesser good must give way

to the greater: Dresden, Hiroshima,

Guantanamo,

and if the total suffering in the world

is the denominator,

then the numerator, your child's suffering,

equals 1.43×10^{-10} of the whole,

roughly.

In the Beginning All Over Again

There's no gainsaying it, I goofed—

next time around, I'll do identity differently:

Released from the clench of sinew and bone,

you'll be carried as the wind lifts strands of hair,

or song, or currents borne from home to porous home,

more moor than mountain,

filling, overflowing, then rising,

circling —sort of like musical chairs,

except now when the music stops,

there'll be room enough for everyone

passing through.

Mika at 14 Months

Mika raises her plump starfish hands,

covers her face, and her mother vanishes—

pulling them apart, wide-eyed with alarm,

she summons Emily from the air,

shrieks, and we clap and cheer,

Yay, Mika! Yay, Mika!

because she shows

what any artist knows:

how just enough tragedy

and just enough applause

make it play.

Pilgrim Soul

Thread thin, they waver

legs like an airy voice

up a scale

ascending the stairs

newly made

like a spider web

or a vine

grows up to a green valley

grows like Jacob's Ladder

where her father tells her,

"If you don't blink, you'll see the angel."

But now, years later, she wakes to the words,

"A good walking stick,

sturdy boots, warm gloves,

and a hat."

Anna's Tricycle

This morning, revising a few poems from the new manuscript,
light pools slowly on my mother Anna's Persian rug,
scattering under her great-granddaughter's tricycle
which rests between the love seat Mother covered
over a half-century ago in a pale yellow fabric and the ebony spinet
upon which sits "The Fireside Book of Folk Songs"
she played from winter evenings,
my sisters and I next to her on the piano bench,
my father, in that same yellow love seat, reading his AMA journal,
looking up at us from time to time, our quavery voices singing
"Joe Hill," "Skye Boat Song," "The Four Insurgent Generals"—
Visiting this afternoon, Anna pedals down the street
singing "Buffalo Gals" at the top of her lungs,
Grandpa trying to keep up,
and as their shadows disappear into the fading light,
I wonder what it is she carries back to us—
those doubled gyres revolving in darkness—
returning what we need
for writing the sun up, riding its great arc,
and for singing it down
again.

Even Now

after a long marriage

I cannot put my finger on just

what makes it work

but this morning my husband asked me,

about the tea he was making,

Do you want it piping hot?

Gingerly drinkable?

Or just drinkable?

Celebrating Shabbat with Irving, our daughter Emily, and granddaughter Mika at Mika's nursery school.

Picknicking in the park with our daughter Claire and granddaughter Anna.

About the Author

Under the Sign of the Samovar is Marcia Katz Wolf's fourth book. Her first collection of poetry, *River, Rivers,* was published in 1996; the second, *Inheritance,* in 2006; and the third, *The Grandmother Poems,* in 2008. First a music therapist and then a teacher, she retired several years ago to spend more time with her family and on her writing. She lives with her husband in Palo Alto.

www.ingramcontent.com/pod-product-compliance
Lightning Source LLC
Chambersburg PA
CBHW052114070526
44584CB00017B/2477